Marion Deuchars

Let's make some GREAT FINGERPRINT ART

LAURENCE KING

PUBLISHED IN 2012 by

LAURENCE KING PUBLISHING Ltd
361 - 373 CITY ROAD
LONDON EC1V 1LR
Tel + 44 20 7841 6900
Fax + 44 20 7841 6910
www. laurenceking.com
enquiries @ Laurenceking.com

Reprinted in 2015

A CATALOGUE RECORD OF THIS BOOK IS AVAILABLE
FROM THE BRITISH LIBRARY.

ISBN 978-1-78067-0-157

Printed in China

for

A

This BOOK belongs to

to

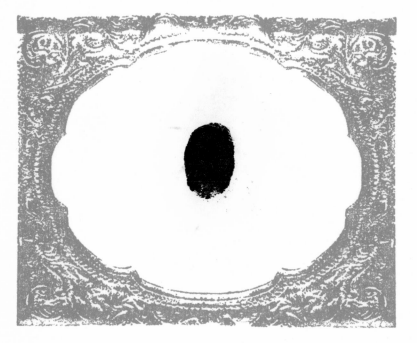

Put your fingerprint in here.

Everything
starts
from a dot

Wassilly Kandinsky

FINGERPRINT FACTS

FINGERPRINTS ARE FORMED BEFORE BIRTH.

WE HAVE RIDGES ON OUR FINGERPRINTS, THESE HELP *
TO IDENTIFY US AS EACH ONE OF THEM IS UNIQUE.

THE RIDGES ALSO GIVE OUR FINGERS THE ROUGH
SURFACE WE NEED TO HOLD A PENCIL OR PICK
UP A BALL.

* NO TWO PEOPLE HAVE EXACTLY THE SAME
FINGERPRINTS - EVEN SIAMESE TWINS.

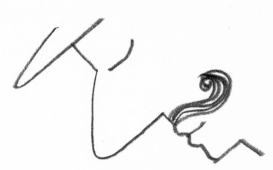

A fingerprint can tell you a lot about the person, such as what age they are, their height and whether they are male or female.

FINGERPRINTS LEAVE THEIR INVISIBLE MARK *
ON THINGS WE TOUCH. COLLECTED AT A CRIME
SCENE, THE POLICE CAN DE-CODE THIS
MARK WITH SPECIAL TOOLS AND EQUIPMENT.

IT HAS BEEN ONE OF THE MOST RELIABLE WAYS
TO CATCH A CRIMINAL SINCE 1915!

* OILS & SWEAT

← RAISED RIDGES. Sometimes known as "DERMAL RIDGES"

EVIDENCE

MAKE YOUR FINGERPRINTS HERE.
WHAT PATTERNS DO YOU SEE? ↙

WHAT **TOOLS** DO YOU NEED TO MAKE

THE BASICS

- INK PADS
- PENCILS
- PAPER
- PAPER TOWEL OR DAMP CLOTH

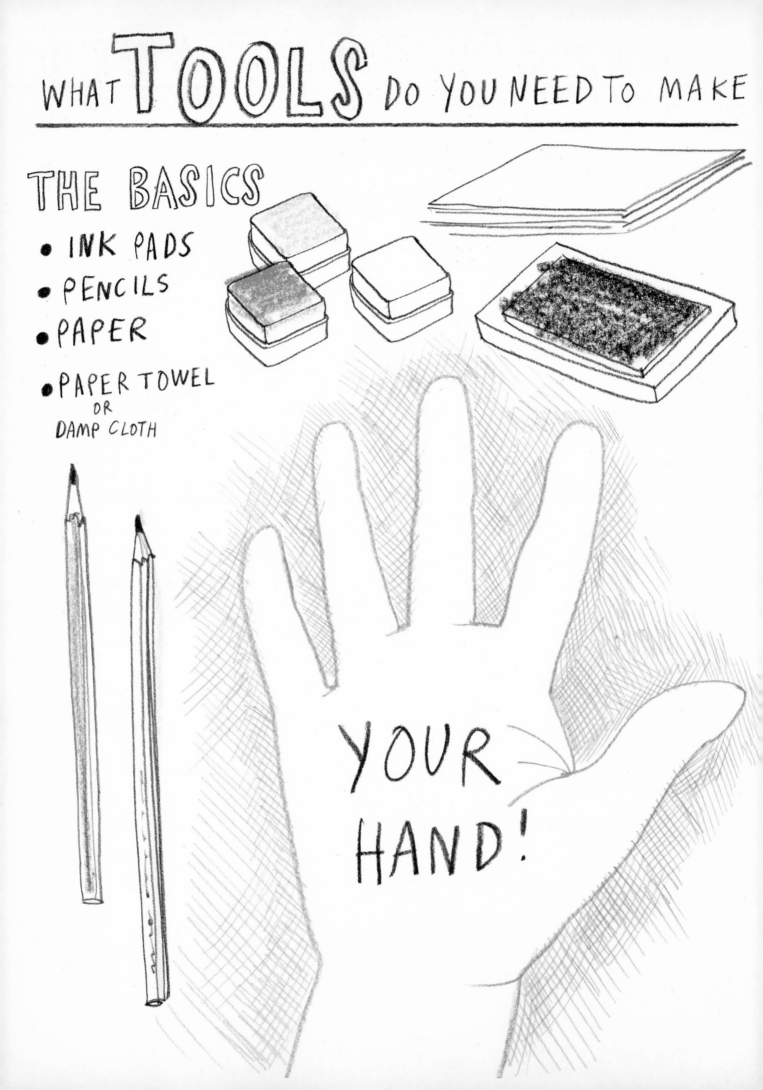

YOUR HAND!

FINGERPRINT ART?

OTHER ART MATERIALS USED IN THIS BOOK

- SCISSORS
- CONSTRUCTION PAPER (in different colours)
- A STRAW
- COLOURED PENCILS AND PENS
- PAINTS (POSTER/CRAFT)
- PENCIL SHARPENER
- WATER CONTAINER
- WHITE GLUE (OR GLUE STICK)
- FELT-TIP PENS
- REMOVABLE TAPE
- PAINT ROLLERS
- COLOURED INK

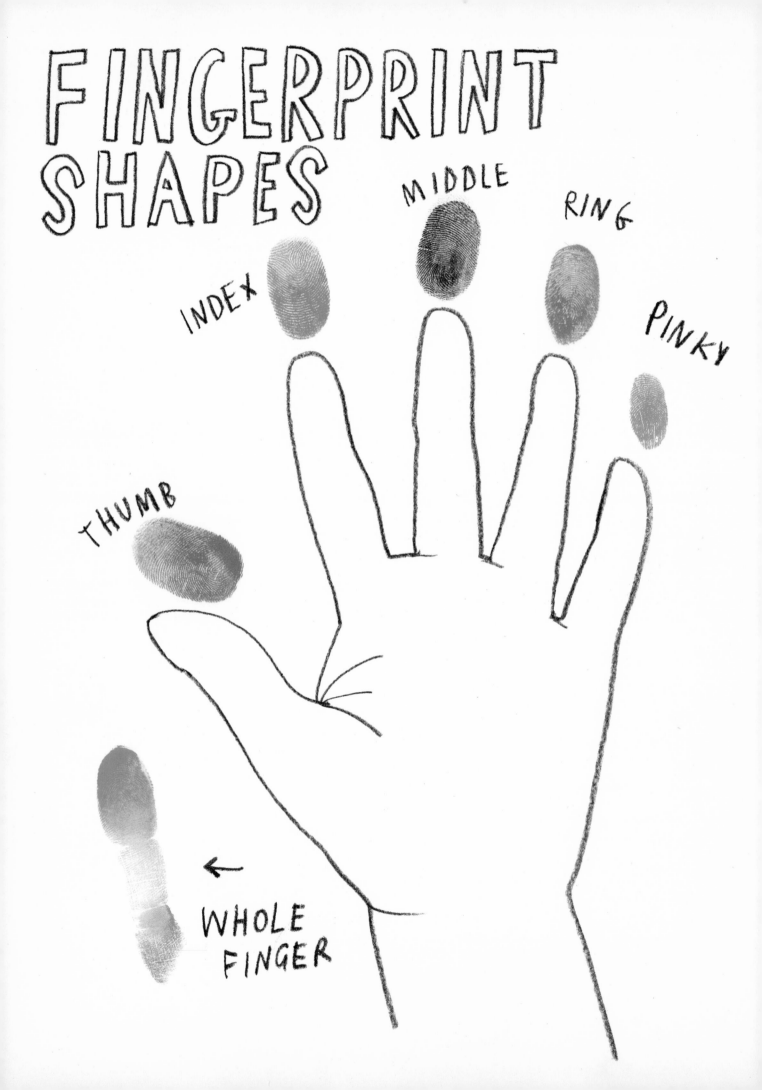

SIMPLE FORMS
WITH THESE SHAPES YOU CAN MAKE ANYTHING.

CIRCLE

HALF OVAL

TRIANGLE

SQUARE OR RECTANGLE

 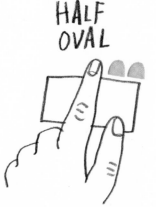  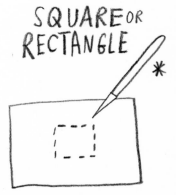

Use the TOP of your finger to make a circle.

Use a piece of paper to make an edge and half-oval print.

Make a stencil with pieces of paper to make differently-shaped prints.

Cut out a shape in a piece of paper to make a stencil.
* Use a craft knife.

* HANDY TIPS *

- Use ONE HAND for fingerprinting and the other hand for drawing.
- To keep your INK PADS CLEAN, wipe fingers on a DAMP CLOTH before changing colour.

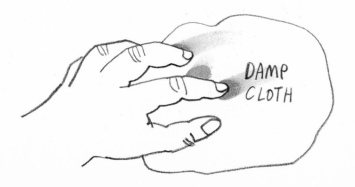

DAMP CLOTH

HAPPY   SAD   CRAZY

THINKING   SCARED   SILLY

SLEEPING   EXCITED   CONFUSED

DELIRIOUS   ANGRY   ALERT

Make your own fingerprints and responses to the expressions.

HAPPY   SAD   CRAZY

THINKING   SCARED   SILLY

SLEEPING   EXCITED   CONFUSED

DELIRIOUS   ANGRY   ALERT

Simple Creatures

Now make your own ↓

pig

turtle

cat

dog

racoon

owl

frog

mouse

some other ideas

chick

bird

fox

sleeping dog

Make fingerprint EYES on BEAR so he is LOOKING at BIRD.

Can you COPY these fingerprint

Characters?

HOW to MAKE Black on White EYES

(like the caterpillar and monkeys)

OPTION 1. Use white ink or paint, or white pencil.*

OPTION 2. Draw eyes on white paper with black pen. Cut them out and then glue onto DRY fingerprint.

draw EYES →

CUT ON OUTSIDE LINE

GLUE → STICK

*

(a china marker is best)

SPRING TREE

MAKE the LEAVES on the TREE.

AUTUMN TREE

MAKE the LEAVES on the TREE.

BEES ARE

Make more leaves on the tree.

HOW to MAKE the BEES.

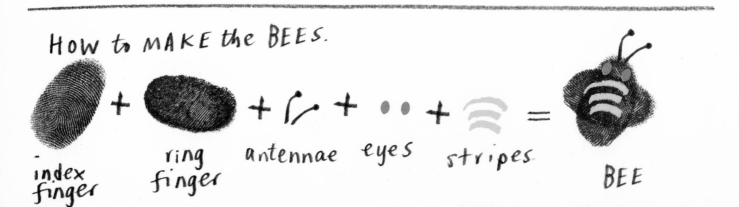

index finger + ring finger + antennae + eyes + stripes = BEE

EVERYWHERE !

FILL THE PAGE WITH BEES.

Add more flowers.

CONTINUE the PATTERN of FLOWERS.

Try different colours.

CUT paper and FINGERPRINTS

WHAT YOU NEED

COLOURED PAPER
GLUE
SCISSORS
INK PADS
FINGERS
PENCIL or PEN

CUT OUT SMALL RANDOM SHAPES
OF COLOURED PAPER AND STICK
THEM ONTO A LARGER PIECE OF
WHITE PAPER.
ADD YOUR FINGERPRINTS
ON THE EMPTY SHAPES.
TO MAKE YOUR OWN CHARACTERS
USE HALF-OVALS AND DIFFERENT
FINGERS.
YOU CAN ALSO ADD DRAWING!

HIDING

USING A PIECE OF PAPER AS A TEMPLATE.
MAKE SOME HALF-OVAL HIDDEN CHARACTERS.

PRINTING
with rubbish:

old magazine

paint or ink

DIP in Paint
Print CIRCLES

PRINT KITCHEN ROLLS,
OLD CARD, PLASTIC LIDS
to make interesting marks
to go alongside your FINGERPRINTS.

Kitchen roll

WHAT YOU WILL NEED

RECYCLED RUBBISH
POSTER PAINT or INK
PAPER PALETTE or OLD
  NEWSPAPER
BRUSH or STICK

old square lid

MARK MAKING WITH CARD

CARD

Dip in Paint

old plastic container or old magazine

PRINT LINES

CARD

Bend the Card to make shapes

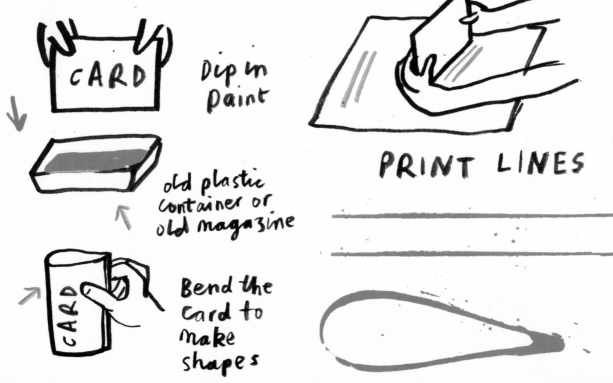

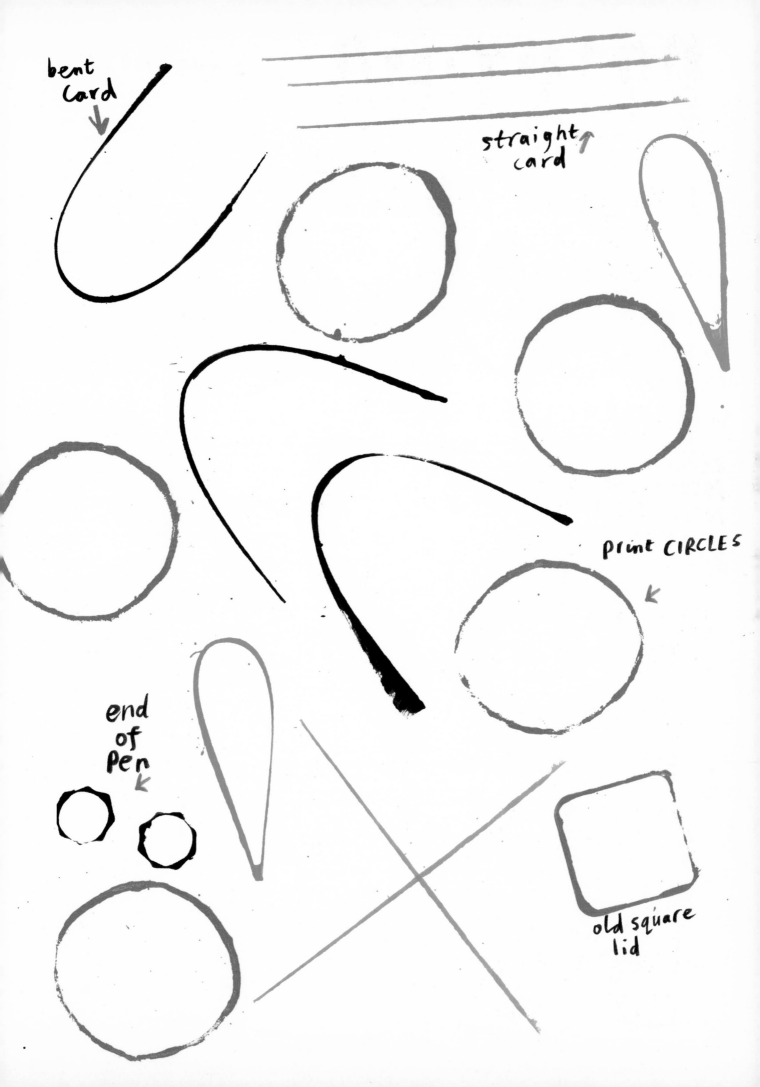

bent
Card

straight
card

print CIRCLES

end
of
pen

old square
lid

PRINTING with rubbish:
CIRCLES, SQUARES, LINES, HOOPS
and fingerprints.

PRINTING with rubbish

CIRCLES, SQUARES, LINES, HOOPS
and fingerprints.

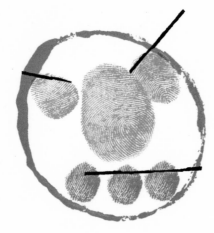

NOW IT'S YOUR TURN!

Handprint
BIRDS

paint

newspaper ↑

WHAT YOU NEED:
- POSTER OR TEMPERA PAINT in a few colours
- FINE PAINTBRUSH for BIRD details
- Medium PAINTBRUSH for painting different colours on FINGERS
- AN OLD MAGAZINE or newspaper

Handprint
BIRDS

Make your own birds.

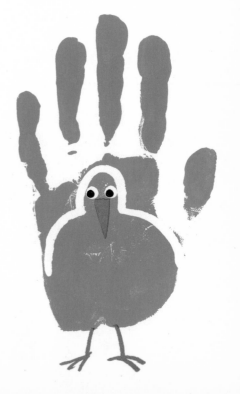

HANDPRINT ANIMALS

leopard

reindeer

zebra

Lions

CRAB

1. Fold a PIECE of and MAKE a HANDPRINT DRIES, fold the paper open carefully to see a

2. add CLAWS, eyes & antennae to MAKE a CRAB

coloured paper in HALF on ONE SIDE. Before it in HALF. and PRESS firmly. mirror-image HANDPRINT.

Elephant

Aliens and Monsters

ADD your THUMBPRINTS here. ↙

NOW try TO MAKE YOUR OWN Aliens and Monsters.

CREATE your own ALIEN

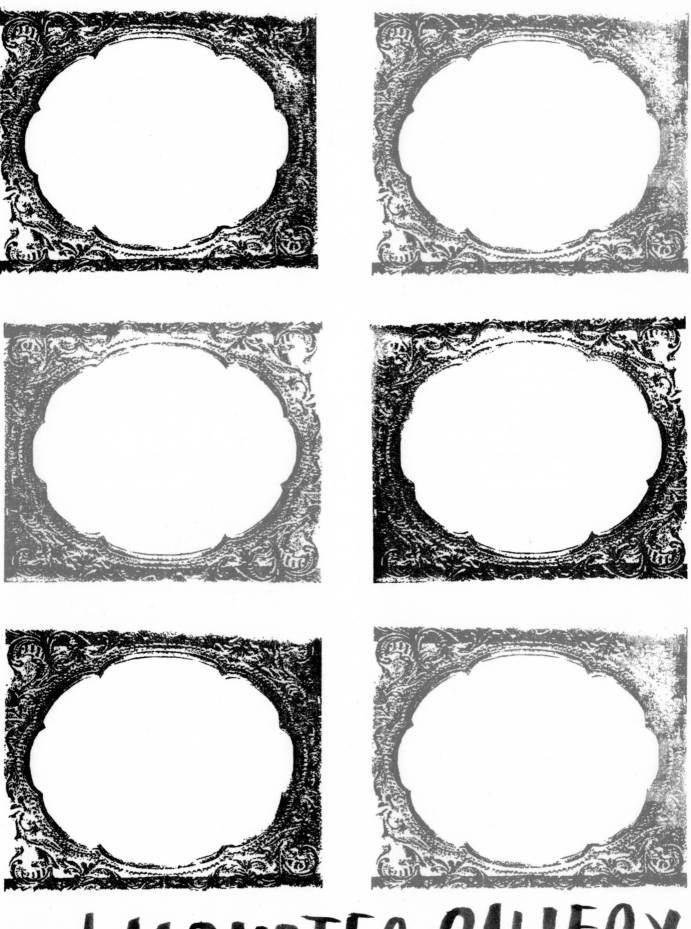

and MONSTER GALLERY.

BLOW PAINTING
AND FINGERPRINTS TO MAKE STRANGE CREATURES.

WHAT YOU NEED

INK
INK PADS
PAPER
STRAW
EYE DROPPER
(MANY INK BOTTLES
HAVE ONE IN THE LID)
PENCILS & PENS

DROP SMALL BLOBS OF
INK ONTO THE PAPER.
BLOW THROUGH THE STRAW
TO MAKE THE INK OR PAINT MOVE
AROUND AND MAKE SOME
INTERESTING SHAPES.
ONCE DRY, ADD FINGERPRINTS
AND DRAW ARMS, LEGS and EYES.

* <u>HANDY TIP</u> *

To make white fingerprint
eyes use a white inkpad or
white poster paint.

NOW try TO MAKE YOUR OWN.

NOW try TO MAKE YOUR OWN.

THE CROCODILE IS DREAMING OF HIS favourite food.

Make your favourite food. ↑

WHITE

USE A WHITE INK PAD OR WHITE POSTER PAINT ON BLACK PAPER TO GET A REVERSE PRINT EFFECT.

YOU WILL ALSO NEED BLACK AND WHITE PENCILS*AND PENS FOR THE DETAILS.

* CHINA WHITE PENCILS ARE BEST.

WHITE on BLACK

ADD your DRAWINGS here.

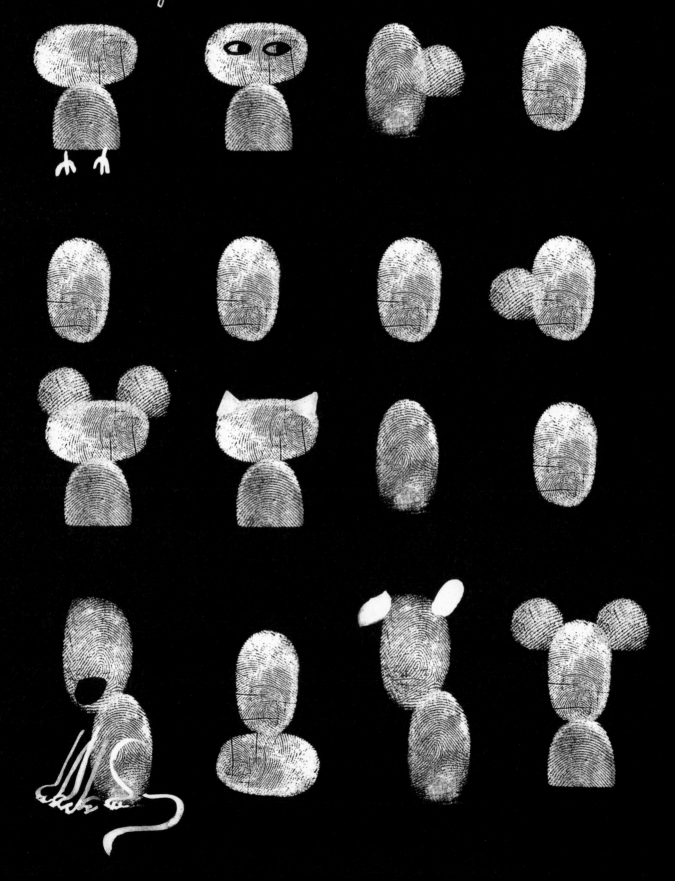

DINOSAURS

TYRANNOSAURUS-REX

VELOCIRAPTOR

STEGOSAURUS

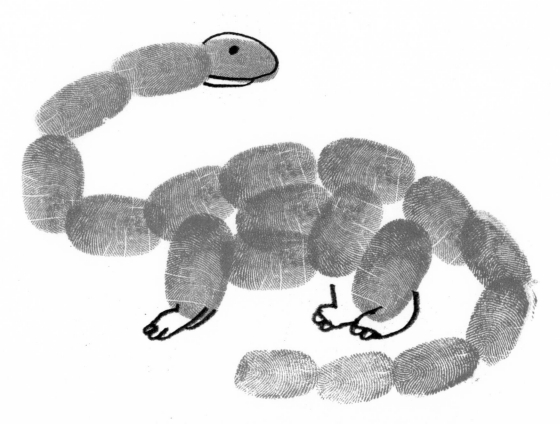

BRACHIOSAURUS

DINOSAURS

TYRANNOSAURUS-REX

VELOCIRAPTOR

NOW TRY TO MAKE THESE DINOSAURS.

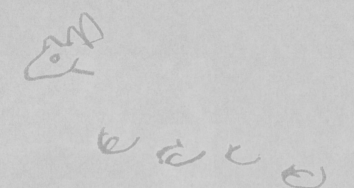

STEGOSAURUS

BRACHIOSAURUS

STENCILS AND FINGERPRINTS.

WHAT YOU NEED

PAPER
SCISSORS
PENCIL
INK PADS

COLOURED PAPER

1. DRAW OR TRACE A
GREYHOUND DOG ON
PAPER.

2 NOW CAREFULLY CUT IT OUT.

3 PLACE STENCIL ON TOP
OF ANOTHER SHEET OF PAPER.
NOW FINGERPRINT THE DOG
SHAPE.

4. GENTLY TAKE AWAY
STENCIL TO REVEAL
YOUR FINGERPRINT
DOG.

GREYHOUND DOG

TRY DIFFERENT
VARIATIONS BY CHANGING
WHERE YOU FINGERPRINT.

STENCILS AND FINGERPRINTS.

AS AN ALTERNATIVE

CUT TWO STENCILS FROM PAPER.
ONCE YOU HAVE MADE THE FINGERPRINTS
WITH ONE STENCIL, USE THE OTHER
TO FRAME IT FOR A DIFFERENT EFFECT.

GIRAFFE

COPY (OR TRACE) THESE STENCILS.
FINGERPRINT ON TOP.

BIG CAT

EXPERIMENT MAKING DIFFERENT BIG CATS.
TRY A LION OR A LEOPARD.
HERE IS A PANTHER.

HOW TO MAKE
TIGER
STRIPES.

CUT A TRIANGLE FROM A
SMALL PIECE OF PAPER.
USE IT AS A FINGERPRINT
STENCIL TO GIVE THE TIGER
HIS STRIPES.

FINGERPRINT
LETTERS OF THE ALPHABET.

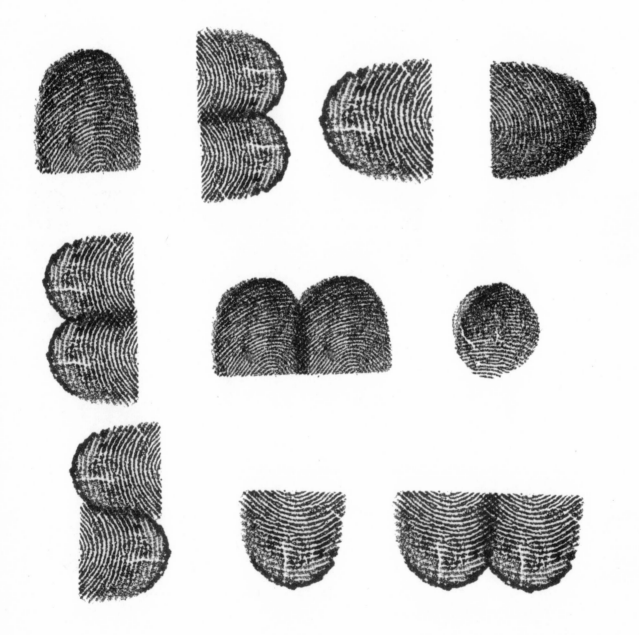

FINGERPRINT
LETTERS OF THE ALPHABET.

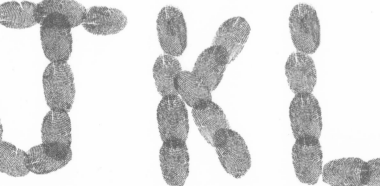

SEE WHAT  LETTERS
YOU CAN MAKE.

Continue this REPEAT PATTERN.

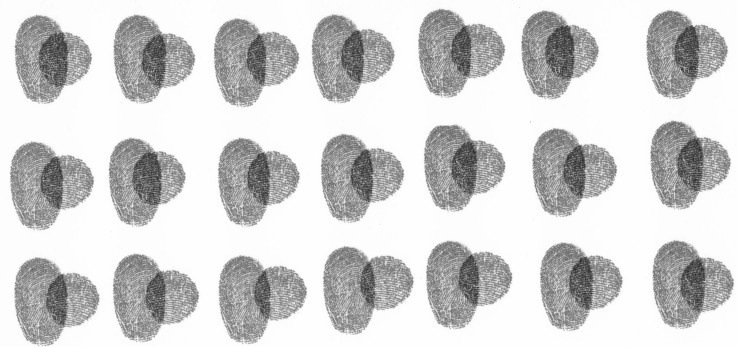

Now make your own pattern.

FLAGS

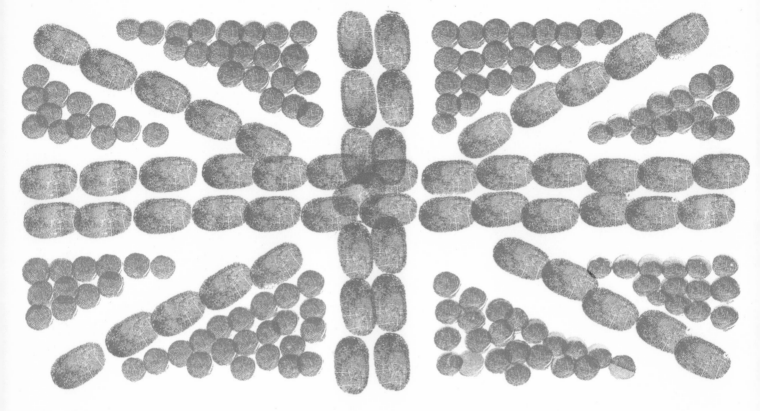

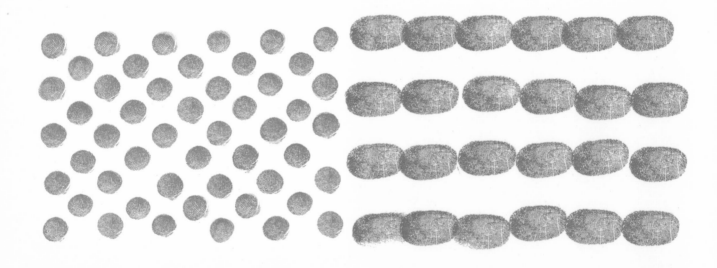

MAKE YOUR OWN FLAGS.

FINISH the PATH so that the DOG

CAN GET to HIS HOME.

DRAW ITS HOME.
IT'S A VERY RICH DOG.

Monkey is scared OF THE SPIDER.
Make some other things you think he might
be scared of.

↓

ADD MORE leaves on the tree to make

You can also make your own bird and hide him too.

the BIRD camouflaged (hidden).

ADD YOUR FINGERPRINT BETWEEN THE TWO SHAPES.

Do it carefully. It should look like it is being held up by the two shapes.

TOTEM POLES

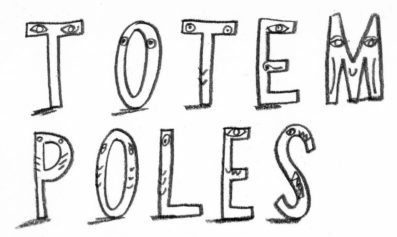

ARE HUGE SCULPTURES CARVED
FROM TREES BY NATIVE AMERICANS.
THEY CAN REPRESENT A FAMILY'S
HISTORY, STORIES AND EXPERIENCES.

DESIGN POLES USING STRANGE CREATURES, ANIMALS AND BIRDS. YOU CAN TELL A STORY ABOUT YOUR OWN FAMILY USING A PET, TEDDY BEAR OR FAVOURITE ZOO ANIMAL.

YOU CAN SEE TOTEM POLES
(sometimes called MEMORIAL POLES.)
IN MANY MUSEUMS.

SKELETONS and SKULLS

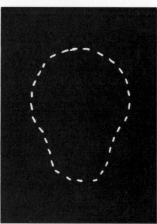

CUT OUT A SKULL SHAPE FROM COLOURED PAPER.

STICK DOWN ON WHITE PAPER.

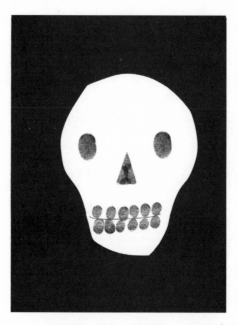

FINGERPRINT EYES, NOSE AND MOUTH TO MAKE A SKULL.

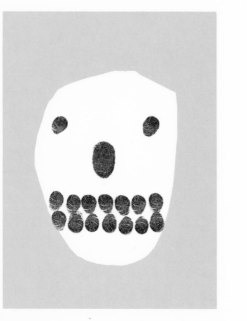

TRY DIFFERENT FACES.

MAKE A WHOLE SKELETON USING FINGERPRINTS!
ADD DETAILS BY DRAWING WITH WHITE INK OR PAINT.

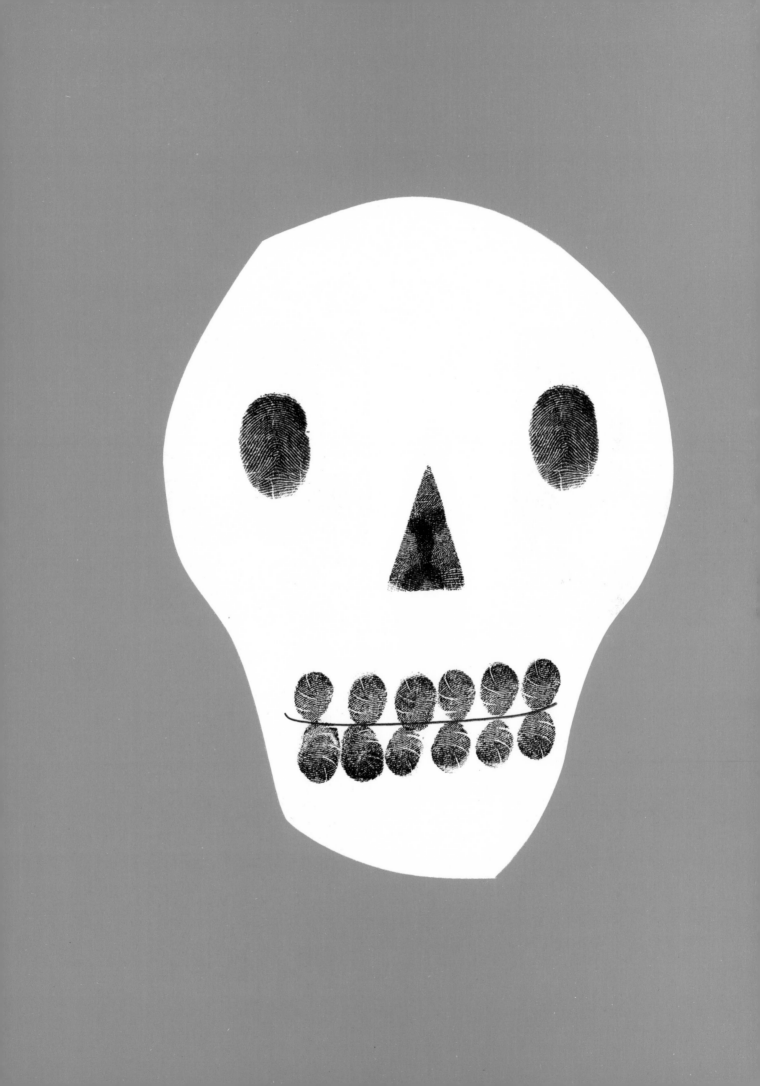

THE DAY OF THE DEAD IS A MEXICAN
HOLIDAY WHICH FOCUSES ON REMEMBERING
WITH LOVE THOSE WHO HAVE DIED.
IT IS A HAPPY DAY, PEOPLE DRESS UP AS
SKELETONS. EAT SKULL SWEETS AND HAVE
SKELETON PARTIES.

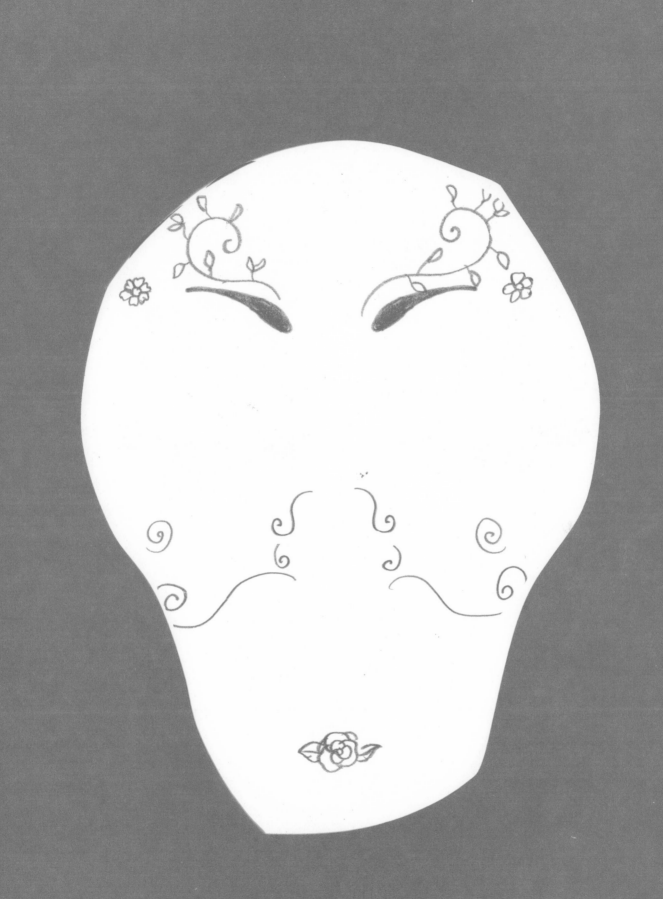

FINGERPRINT EYES, NOSE AND MOUTH.
ADD DECORATION AND COLOUR WITH
FELT-TIP PENS OR COLOURED PENCILS.

MAKE YOUR OWN.

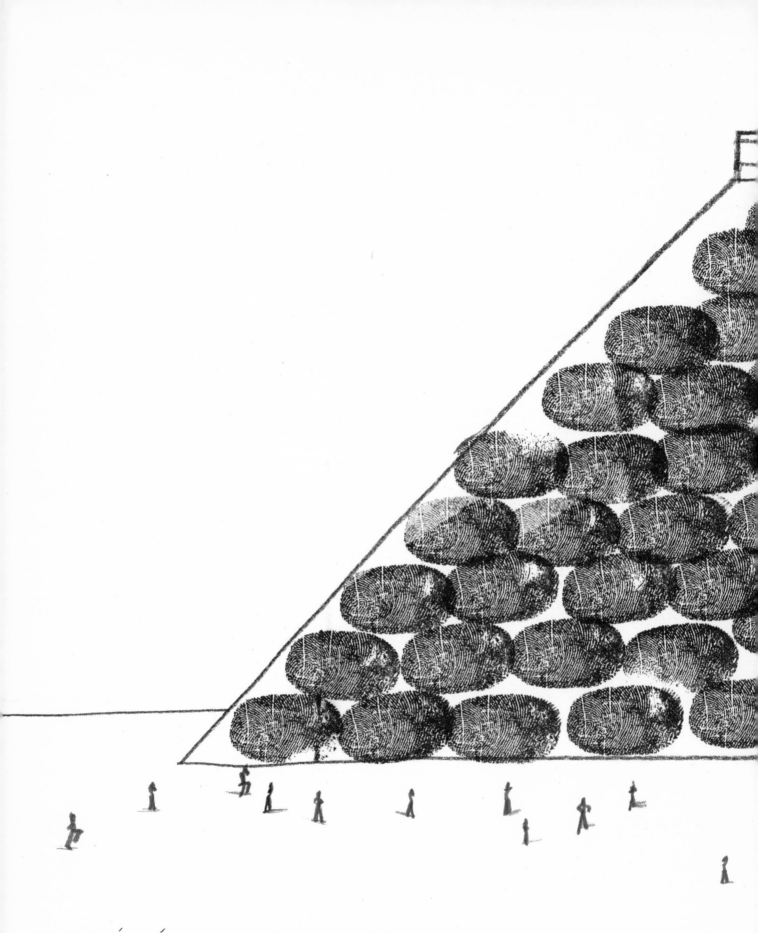

CHICHÉN ITZÁ IS A TEMPLE (OR PYRAMID) IN MEXICO
BUILT BY THE MAYAS! IT IS 75 FEET TALL AND IS
1500 YEARS OLD. THE MAYAS KNEW A LOT
ABOUT THE CALENDAR. ON THE FIRST DAY OF
SPRING, THE SUN CASTS A SHADOW ON THE STEPS
THAT LOOKS LIKE A SNAKE WIGGLING DOWN THE PYRAMID.

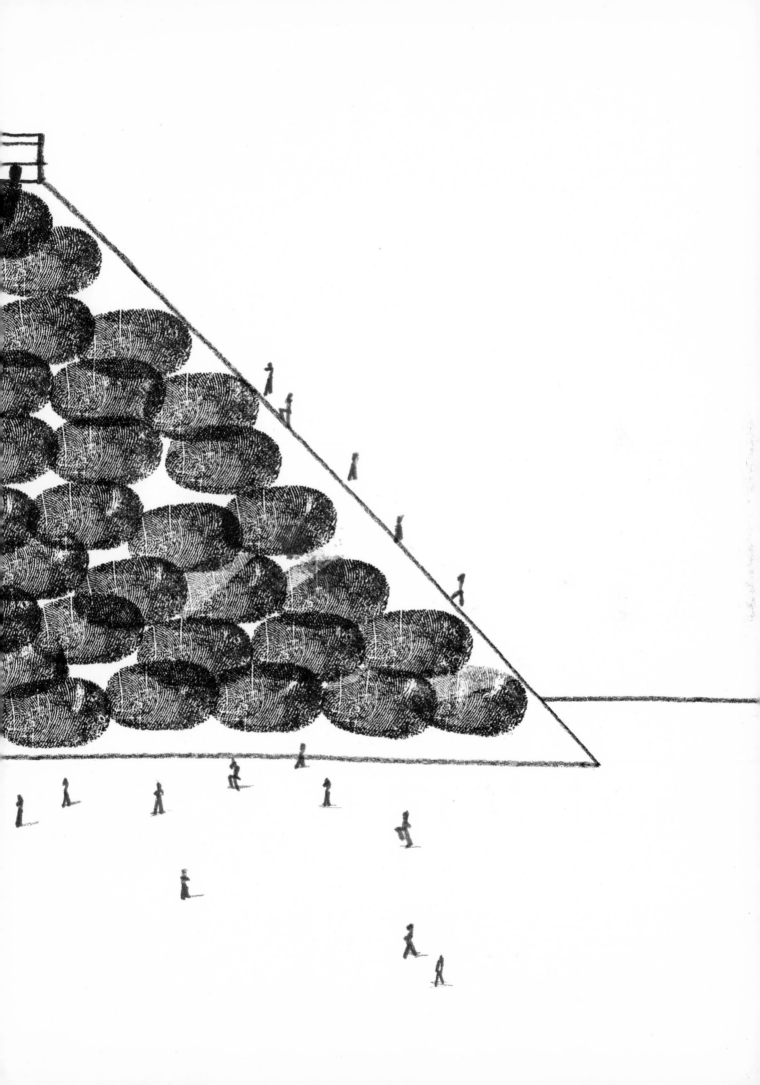

CAN YOU MAKE YOUR OWN PYRAMID AND SMALL PEOPLE?
IF YOU LIKE, DRAW SOME SMALL TREASURE INSIDE,
THEN HIDE IT WITH YOUR FINGERPRINT MARKS.

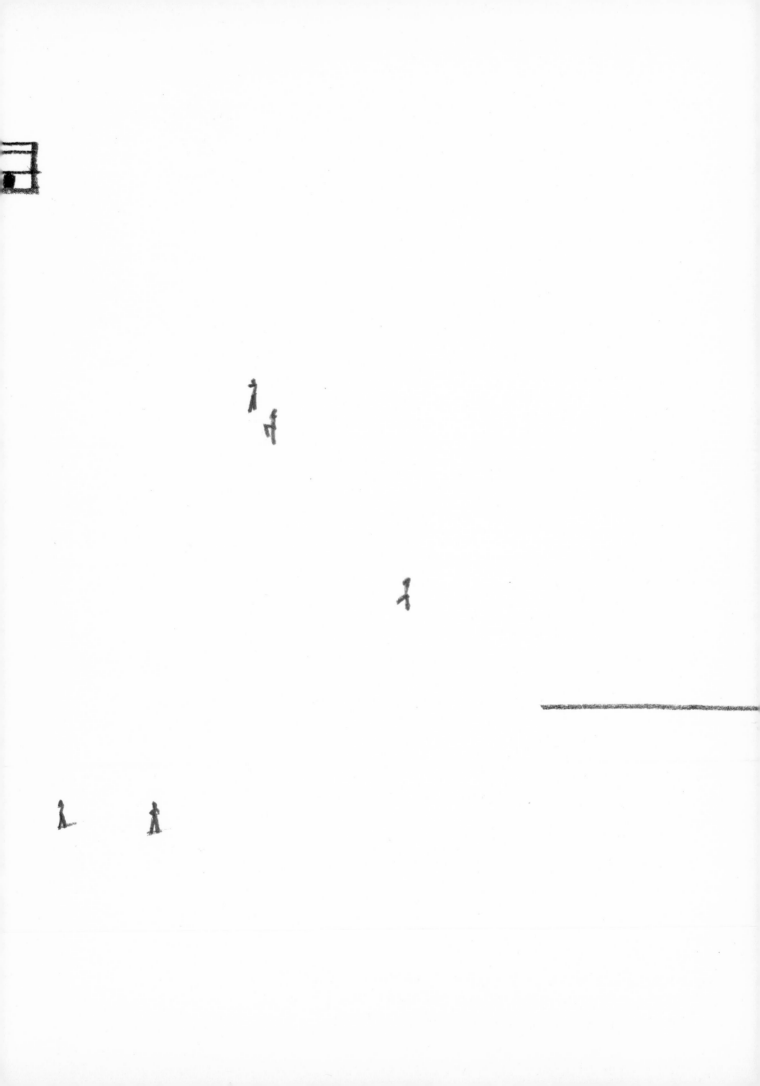

WEIGHT
and BALANCE

HOW HEAVY IS A
FINGERPRINT?

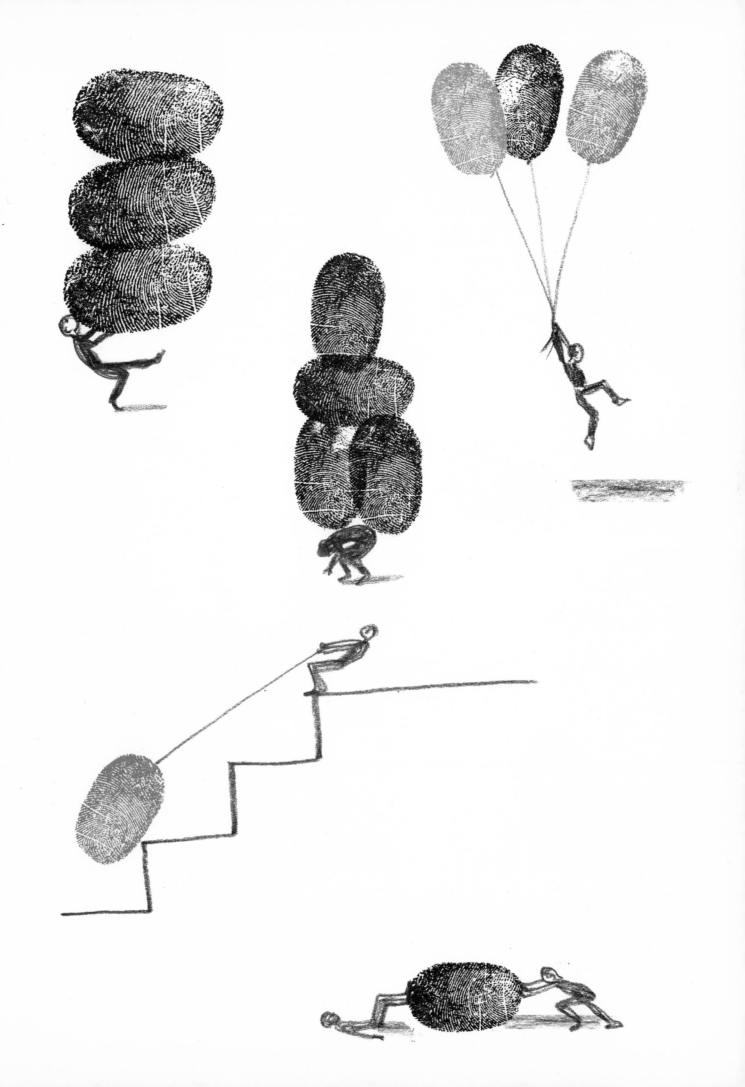

BUILDING
WITH FINGERPRINTS

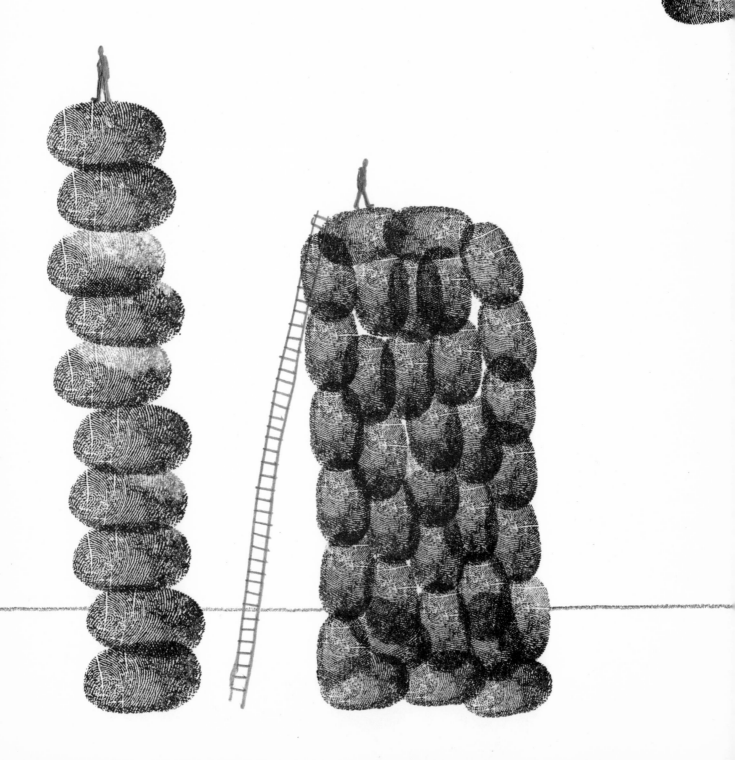

SEE WHAT YOU CAN BUILD.

MAKE the BALLOONS so he can FLY!

HOW WILL THE
BIRD REACH THE
WATER IN THE
GLASS?

ANSWER

FILL THE GLASS
WITH (FINGERPRINT)
PEBBLES AND THE
WATER WILL RISE
TO THE TOP OF THE GLASS.

HOW CAN YOU PROTECT THE DUCK FROM THE
LION USING FINGERPRINTS?

THE RACE

Add your own runners to the RACE.

THE DANCE

Add your own DANCERS.

FAST

PRESS THEN DRAG
TO MAKE A SMUDGE.

NOW YOU HAVE
A "FAST"
FINGERPRINT.

Make more
fast things.

SLOW

make some
slow things.

and finally.....

AN ENORMOUS
THANK YOU to

Hamish and Alexander for
their inspiration and energy. ♡

Angus Hyland
'my inspiration'.

M. Deuchars (Snr)

Laurence King
Jo Lightfoot
Donald Dinwiddie
Felicity Awdry

Mark Cass for
continuous support and
friendship.
www.cassart.co.uk

Mathew and the wonderful team at
www.withassociates.com

Jason Godfrey
www.godfreydesign.co.uk

Heart Agency
Darrel, Helen, Amanda,
Chloe and Jenny
www.heartagency.com

www.mariondeuchars.com